UNPLUG

BREATHE

CREATE

A MONTH OF
CLAIMING YOUR CREATIVE
SPACE THROUGH MEDITATION

Unplug Breathe Create: A Month of Claiming Your Creative Space Through Meditation is a work of my own creation.

The information in this book was correct at the time of publication, and the Author does not assume any liability for loss or damage caused by errors or omissions, again, this is my perspective, opinion, and experience, so it has been written as such.

ISBN - 979-8-9865393-6-2

Cover, Book Design, and Layout by megs thompson, megswrites llc
www.megswrites.com

in omnia paratus
publishing

www.inomniaparatuspublishing.com

"TO BE CREATIVE YOU MUST CREATE A SPACE FOR YOURSELF WHERE YOU CAN BE UNDISTURBED... SEPARATE FROM EVERYDAY CONCERNS."

—JOHN CLEESE

This journal is part of the UNPLUG BREATHE CREATE series & designed to be used alongside a bespoke guided meditation.

Download this month's meditation using the QR code below:

HOW TO BEST USE THIS JOURNAL & MEDITATION

UNPLUG

The first step to reconnecting with ourselves as creative beings is to unplug & disconnect even temporarily from the countless electronic tethers that keep us firmly held in the world of shoulds & must's.

BREATHE

Take a few deep breaths, paying close attention to the way oxygen moves through your mouth & nose, filling your lungs & reawakening the creative genius locked safely within you, exhaling any fears, hesitations, or doubts that may filter your magic.

CREATE

Release your desire to control, plan & perfect every step & movement you make. Embrace the often wild, messy & chaotic magic that comes with allowing your inner creative to explore & play. Prepare yourself to experience fulfillment & satisfaction in new & creative ways.

DAILY ROUTINE

While moving through your day, begin implementing the use of affirmations. Both habits & beliefs are formed & strengthened through consistent repetition & before you know it your thoughts will become truths.

Included below are powerful affirmations that when paired with your daily tasks & activities, will empower you through this month of finding & claiming your own creative space.

I recommend repeating one or more of these affirmations aloud anytime you find yourself in front of a mirror, washing your hands, or refilling your beverage of choice.

I AM NATURALLY CREATIVE.

I AM CONFIDENT IN MY UNIQUE BRILLIANCE.

I AM A TRENDSETTER.

30-DAY ENERGY TRACKER

When you've completed your daily meditation, make note of a single word or phrase that best describes your energy level in that moment.

Day 1	Day 2	Day 3	Day 4	Day 5
Day 6	Day 7	Day 8	Day 9	Day 10
Day 11	Day 12	Day 13	Day 14	Day 15
Day 16	Day 17	Day 18	Day 19	Day 20
Day 21	Day 22	Day 23	Day 24	Day 25
Day 26	Day 27	Day 28	Day 29	Day 30

DAY 1

Where do you feel most creative? Is there a space within your home? Outdoors? Describe this space in detail. What is it about this space that you find most appealing?

ON A SCALE OF 1-5 WHAT'S YOUR
CURRENT CREATIVITY LEVEL?

DAY 2

Did you have a special space that was your own as a child? Perhaps a treehouse, corner of your bedroom, hidden behind a couch, or a clubhouse in the backyard. What was it about this space that you were most drawn to?

DAY 3

Where do you spend your creative time currently? Do you have a home office, dedicated craft space, or designated space within a shared room of the house? Is this a space you share with others or can use without interruption?

DAY 4

When do you feel most creatively confident? This may be when you're playing with words, music, paint, food, dance, clay, wood, steel, yarn, etc. Describe how you feel.

ON A SCALE OF 1-5 WHAT'S YOUR
CURRENT CREATIVITY LEVEL?

DAY 5

Describe in detail the creative space you visualize during this month's guided meditation. Where is it? How does it feel? Smell? What sounds do you hear?

DAY 6

Looking back at the space you described on Day 5, how might you go about creating that space in your daily life? Is this a place that already exists?

ON A SCALE OF 1-5 WHAT'S YOUR
CURRENT CREATIVITY LEVEL?

DAY 7

What are 3 aspects of your daily life that bring you the most joy. How might you increase the creativity associated with these three tasks/situations/experiences?

DAY 8

If you were to write a short story with yourself as the main character, where would the story take place? Would you exist as you do now, or would you take a different form?

ON A SCALE OF 1-5 WHAT'S YOUR
CURRENT CREATIVITY LEVEL?

DAY 9

How confident are you when it comes to writing creatively? Is this a practice you enjoy, something you'd like to explore, or an idea that leaves you feeling anxious?

ON A SCALE OF 1-5 WHAT'S YOUR
CURRENT CREATIVITY LEVEL?

DAY 10

Close your eyes. Take 3 deep breaths & ask yourself, how do I want to explore my creativity today? What answer do you receive? How comfortable are you with trusting your intuition to guide your creativity?

ON A SCALE OF 1-5 WHAT'S YOUR
CURRENT CREATIVITY LEVEL?

DAY 11

When was the last time you created something for fun, without purpose or direction? How confident did you feel? What did you enjoy most about the process? What hesitations did you experience?

ON A SCALE OF 1-5 WHAT'S YOUR
CURRENT CREATIVITY LEVEL?

DAY 12

Write a short love letter or note to your ideal creative space, or favorite creative tool/material.

ON A SCALE OF 1-5 WHAT'S YOUR
CURRENT CREATIVITY LEVEL?

DAY 13

What place or space gives you the most peace & clarity? Describe this place or space using all of your senses, in as much detail as possible.

ON A SCALE OF 1-5 WHAT'S YOUR
CURRENT CREATIVITY LEVEL?

DAY 14

Today's prompt is a little different. Set a timer for 5 minutes & doodle in each of the areas below, utilizing the partial shapes provided. When time is up, look back at your creations & make note of any themes. Perhaps there's a bigger project hidden within one of your tiny bits of creative genius.

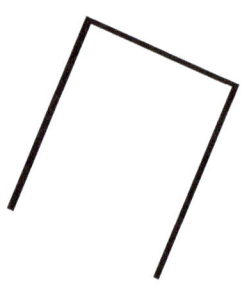

ON A SCALE OF 1-5 WHAT'S YOUR
CURRENT CREATIVITY LEVEL?

DAY 15

Who do you consider to be the most creative person you know? What is it about them that makes you feel this way? Are these attributes or traits things they've learned, or are they innately natural?

_____

_____

_____

_____

_____

_____

_____

_____

_____

_____

_____

_____

_____

_____

_____

_____

_____

ON A SCALE OF 1-5 WHAT'S YOUR
CURRENT CREATIVITY LEVEL?

DAY 16

Failure is a part of life, it's also part of the creative process. When did you last fail during a creative project? Focus on the fact that while the outcome may have fallen short of your intention, it was temporary & there is no reason to not try again.

ON A SCALE OF 1-5 WHAT'S YOUR
CURRENT CREATIVITY LEVEL?

DAY 17

How often do you allow yourself to embrace your own creativity? What's holding you back from prioritizing this time? As with any habit or skill, consistent repetition strengthens & solidifies your confidence as a creative being. Are you able to set aside 10, 20, or even 30 minutes each day to explore your creativity?

ON A SCALE OF 1-5 WHAT'S YOUR
CURRENT CREATIVITY LEVEL?

DAY 18

What are 3 traits that set you apart from others?
Think of things that make you the unique individual
you are. How do these attributes serve you? How do
they limit you?

_____

_____

_____

_____

_____

_____

_____

_____

_____

_____

_____

_____

_____

_____

_____

_____

_____

_____

ON A SCALE OF 1-5 WHAT'S YOUR CURRENT CREATIVITY LEVEL?

DAY 19

What sounds, smells, colors, temperatures, or environments most ignite your creative confidence? Do you have a specific soundtrack you like to listen to, or a candle you light?

ON A SCALE OF 1-5 WHAT'S YOUR
CURRENT CREATIVITY LEVEL?

DAY 20

What's your personal superpower? If you aren't able to think of something, ask a friend or family member to share what they see as your superpower. How are you using this skill in your daily life?

ON A SCALE OF 1-5 WHAT'S YOUR
CURRENT CREATIVITY LEVEL?

DAY 21

Write a letter of gratitude to yourself. Be proud of who you are, the things you've accomplished, and situations you've overcome.

ON A SCALE OF 1-5 WHAT'S YOUR
CURRENT CREATIVITY LEVEL?

DAY 22

What's one activity that cheers you up no matter what else might be going on? When was the last time you enjoyed this activity? What is it about the experience that you enjoy the most?

_____

_____

_____

_____

_____

_____

_____

_____

_____

_____

_____

_____

_____

_____

_____

ON A SCALE OF 1-5 WHAT'S YOUR
CURRENT CREATIVITY LEVEL?

DAY 23

Where do you feel the most resistance when it comes to embracing your own creativity? Are these feelings based in past experiences or assumptions?

ON A SCALE OF 1-5 WHAT'S YOUR
CURRENT CREATIVITY LEVEL?

DAY 24

When do you feel the most creatively confident?

ON A SCALE OF 1-5 WHAT'S YOUR
CURRENT CREATIVITY LEVEL?

DAY 25

What forms of creative expression do you find come most easily, naturally, to you? When do remember first being aware of this ease? How might you apply these same feelings to new forms of creative expression?

_____

_____

_____

_____

_____

_____

_____

_____

_____

_____

_____

_____

_____

_____

ON A SCALE OF 1-5 WHAT'S YOUR
CURRENT CREATIVITY LEVEL?

DAY 26

How would you choose to creatively express yourself today, if time & money weren't factors? What's holding you back from doing so? Is it truly time, money, a fear of failure, or something else?

DAY 27

How are you currently communicating your unique voice, message, or story to others? How might you be able to bring more creativity into this process? What feelings or hesitations do you feel around this?

DAY 28

As children, we're naturally curious & willing to try new things, getting creative even when it may be uncomfortable. How can you embrace your childlike curiosity & creativity now?

ON A SCALE OF 1-5 WHAT'S YOUR
CURRENT CREATIVITY LEVEL?

DAY 29

Oftentimes the key to building creative confidence is maintaining a beginner's mindset, remaining open & curious to the countless solutions surrounding us. How can you better embrace a beginners mindset?

ON A SCALE OF 1-5 WHAT'S YOUR
CURRENT CREATIVITY LEVEL?

DAY 30

When do you feel most creatively confident? Where in your body do you feel this? How would you describe this feeling or sensation? How might you be able to weave this into your daily life?

If you already have an
UNPLUG BREATHE CREATE
subscription, keep an eye on your
mailbox for your next delivery.

If you aren't yet a member but
would like to be, or are
interested in gifting a
membership to someone else,
scan the QR code below.